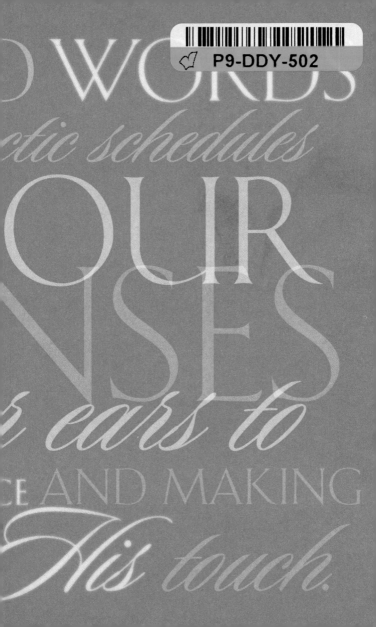

Presented to:

....

By:

....

INTIMACY
with the
ALMIGHTY

ENCOUNTERING
CHRIST IN THE SECRET PLACES
OF YOUR LIFE

CHARLES R. SWINDOLL

J. COUNTRYMAN
NASHVILLE, TENNESEE

Copyright © 1999 by J. Countryman, a division of Thomas Nelson, Inc., Nashville, Tennessee 37214.

Copyright © 1996 by W Publishing, Inc. Dallas, Texas 75039.

Project Editor: Terri Gibbs

All Scripture quotations in this book, except those noted otherwise, are from the New American Standard Bible © 1960, 1962, 1963, 1971, 1972, 1973, 1975, and 1977 by the Lockman Foundation, and are used by permission.

Other Scripture quotations are from the following sources:

The Amplified Bible (AMP). Copyright © 1965 Zondervan Publishing House. Used by permission.

The New International Version of the Bible (NIV), Copyright © 1983 by the Internation Bible Society. Used by permission of Zondervan Bible Publishers.

The New King James Version (NKJV). copyright © 1979, 1980, 1982, Thomas Nelson, Inc. Publisher. Used by permission.

The Good News Bible, Today's English Version (TEV)—Old Testament: Copyright © American Bible Society 1976; New Testament: Copyright © American Bible Society, 1966, 1971, 1976. Used by permission.

The Living Bible (TLB), copyright © 1971 by Tyndale House Publishers. Used by permission.

Designed by David Uttley Design, Sisters, Oregon

ISBN: 0-8499-5610-2

Printed and bound in the United States of America

CONTENTS

6

—

INTRODUCTION

13

—

INTIMACY WITH THE ALMIGHTY

18

—

PAUL'S PASSIONATE PURSUIT

25

—

FOUR DECISIONS...FOUR DISCIPLINES

74

—

CONCLUSION

79

—

NOTES

113555

INTRODUCTION

During this unique period of my life I have been able to enjoy a brief time of relief from the demands of the pastorate. While I have been busy, the deadlines have been less frequent, allowing me more opportunities to think and to record my thoughts. I've loved the change! Much like an interlude in a musical score, it has been a time of quiet and much-needed reflection.

Not only have I been able to catch my breath and do more reading than before, I have also had the opportunity to observe the religious land-scape of our times with greater objectivity. Free from the pressing responsibilities that were part of my life as a pastor for over thirty years, I have found myself more in the role of a listener and learner than a speaker and teacher. It has been an enriching interlude that will surely come to an end in the not-too-distant future.

Certainly, as the Bible teacher on "Insight for Living" and the president of Dallas Theological Seminary, I have had a full plate. The extensive travel and my many new responsibilities have held my feet to the fire. My relationship with a close circle of academic colleagues at the seminary has also enabled me to remain accountable. The new role has been a refreshing one, though not without its own pressures and challenges.

Best of all, I have had the opportunity to look at ministry in general and the church in particular with new eyes . . . to see things I didn't have the time to see before . . . to think about them without frequent interruptions.

While I have missed some aspects of the pastorate, there have been a few things I have not missed at all. I repeat, the two-year interlude has been of inestimable value, especially as I anticipate returning to the role of a shepherd sometime yet future.

One of the growing concerns I have entertained as a result of this temporary time of appraisal is the busyness of so many in the body. Pastors and parishioners alike have often confided in me, admitting that the "tyranny of the urgent" is not a theoretical issue, but a very real fact of life. It leaves them feeling strung out, impatient, occasionally resentful, and even worse, empty. This was the cry of one clergyman who whispered to me following a meeting with pastors, "Nobody around me knows this, but I'm operating on fumes. I am lonely, hollow, shallow, enslaved to a schedule that never lets up." As I embraced him and affirmed his vulnerability and honesty, he began to weep with deep, heaving sobs. We prayed before he slipped back into the crowd.

"Lonely, hollow, shallow, and enslaved to a schedule". . . those words have haunted me for months. I wonder how many who read these pages feel the same. Perhaps you have not expressed your world in those words, but they describe why you feel so frustrated, so frayed.

As a result of my observations and that recent encounter specifically, I decided to do some serious thinking and reading and praying. My journal became the anvil on which most of my private thoughts were hammered out. Thankfully, I have had the time to let those thoughts linger and spawn other thoughts that drove me deeper until I arrived at the heart of what seems to be the core issue—a lack of intimacy. Pure and simple, that best defines the problem: an absence of intimacy with the Almighty. Involvements, yes, but not intimacy. Activities and programs aplenty, but not intimacy.

Once I landed upon it, I decided to face it head-on—in my own life first, then in the lives of fellow believers. My desire was to do more than analyze the problem, though I needed to do that. There must also be a solution—a precise and realistic way of relief—if one hopes to recover from this malady that is reaching epidemic proportions within the family of God.

There is.

That's why I've picked up my pen to write this book.

Hopefully, those who read these pages will find that inner satisfaction is neither complicated nor mystical, but it does call for some radical changes. Difficult changes. Unpopular changes. Lifestyle changes. Essential changes in the secret places of your life.

Without them, however, intimacy with the Almighty remains a distant dream. What's worse, we are left with the frightening alternative: feeling "lonely, hollow, shallow, enslaved to a schedule that never lets up."

Charles Swindoll
Dallas, Texas

INTIMACY
with the
ALMIGHTY

ENCOUNTERING
CHRIST IN THE SECRET PLACES
OF YOUR LIFE

SOME OF
GOD'S BEST TRUTHS,
LIKE PRICELESS
TREASURES, ARE HIDDEN
IN DEPTHS MOST FOLKS
NEVER TAKE THE TIME
TO SEARCH OUT.

INTIMACY WITH THE ALMIGHTY

❧

Deep things are intriguing. Deep jungles. Deep water. Deep caves and canyons. Deep thoughts and conversations.

There is nothing like depth to make us dissatisfied with superficial, shallow things. Once we have delved below the surface and had a taste of the marvels and mysteries of the deep, we realize the value of taking the time and going to the trouble of plumbing those depths.

This is especially true in the spiritual realm. God invites us to go deeper rather than to be content with surface matters. We read in the Scriptures that the Spirit of God "searches all things, even the depths of God" (1 Cor. 2:10). The depth of His wisdom and ways is defined as "unsearchable" and "unfathomable" according to Romans 11:33:

> *Oh, the depth of the riches*
> *both of the wisdom and knowledge of God!*
> *How unsearchable are His judgments*
> *and unfathomable His ways!*

Toward the end of his struggles, Job refers to the Lord's deep, mysterious, and inexplicable purposes as "things too wonderful for me, which I did not know" (Job 42:3). The prophet Daniel stated that God "reveals the profound and hidden things" and that "He knows what is in the darkness" (Dan. 2:22). We read elsewhere "He reveals mysteries from the darkness, and brings the deep darkness into light" (Job 12:22). The psalmist testifies that "Thy judgments are like a great deep" (Ps. 36:6).

Clearly, our Lord operates in realms far beyond our ability to comprehend, but He longs for us to explore and experience that which is beyond the obvious. Some of His best truths, like priceless treasures, are hidden in depths most folks never take the time to search out. Our loss! Patiently and graciously He waits to reveal insights and dimensions of truth to those who care enough to probe, to examine, to ponder.

Such searching is not merely an intellectual pursuit. God's ways are not discovered through the normal, humanistic methods of research.

Can you discover the depths of God?
Can you discover the limits of the Almighty?
They are high as the heavens, what can you do?
Deeper than Sheol, what can you know?

JOB 11:7–8

As important and intriguing as divine depths might be, they defy discovery by the natural means of our minds. He reserves these things for those whose hearts are completely His . . . for those who take the time to wait before Him. Only in that way can there be intimacy with the Almighty.

Tragically, precious little in this hurried and hassled age promotes such intimacy. We have become a body of people who look more like a herd of cattle in a stampede than a flock of God beside green pastures and still waters. Our fore-fathers knew, it seems, how to commune with the Almighty ... but do we? We must learn anew to think deeply, to worship meaningfully, to meditate unhurriedly.

Richard Foster's words penetrate:

Superficiality is the curse of our age. The doctrine of instant satisfaction is a primary spiritual problem. The desperate need today is not for a greater number of intelligent people, or gifted people, but for deep people.[1]

Stop and think about that before going on. Ask yourself a hard question. Be honest in your answer: "Am I among the *deep* people?"

You may not feel as though you are as deep a person as you'd like to be. However, you have some level of interest in becoming so; otherwise, you would not have picked up this book. More than likely, you've grown weary of superficial things . . . you're tired of skating talk and shallow thinking. You know there has to be more; you're just not sure how to get there. One thing is certain: You don't want to stay where you are.

I commend you. No one is ready to take on the depths unless he or she is fed up with the superficial. What you long for, unless I miss my guess, is intimacy with the Almighty. You want to be profoundly aware of His presence, in touch with Him at the deepest possible level, thinking His thoughts, gleaning His wisdom, and living as close to His heart as is humanly possible, operating your life in the nucleus of His will. I desire the same, I freely admit.

PAUL'S PASSIONATE PURSUIT

W hat we long for is to become more deeply and intimately acquainted with Christ. Those are not my words but the words found in the Amplified Bible's rendering of Paul's statement in Philippians 3:10. Read the following words slowly and thoughtfully.

[For my determined purpose is]
that I may know Him—that I may progressively
become more deeply and intimately
acquainted with Him, perceiving and recognizing
and understanding [the wonders of His Person]
more strongly and more clearly.
And that I may in that same way come to
know the power outflowing from
His resurrection [the power it exerts over

believers]; and that I may so share His
sufferings as to be continually transformed
[in spirit into His likeness even]
to His death.

PHILIPPIANS 3:10 AMP

In that single sentence we find the apostle's great goal for life. He refers to it as his "determined purpose" as a follower of the Lord Jesus Christ. What was that? Go back and read the verse again, preferably aloud. Turn the key words over in your mind. Chew on them. Get alone and ponder them:

That I may know Him . . .
 progressively become more deeply
  and intimately acquainted with Him,
   perceiving . . .
    recognizing . . .
     understanding . . .
      continually transformed. . . .

Could anything on this earth be more important for a child of God? I don't think so. Yet, strangely, so few pursue this all-important priority.

A change is in order! Like the great apostle, let's make this our "determined purpose." Let's deliberately embrace this aim: to "become more intimately acquainted with Christ." Not intimately acquainted with theology, as important as theology may be. Not intimately acquainted with the church, as valuable as the church may be. Not with sharing Christ with others, as stimulating and significant as evangelism may be. No, none of the above!

With *Christ*. With Him and Him alone! From this time forward, our goal in life is to become intimately acquainted with Him. I believe this is precisely what Jesus had in mind when He commanded, "Seek first the kingdom of God and His righteousness . . ." (Matt. 6:33 NKJV).

The psalmist understood. He, too, longed for it.

As the deer pants for the water brooks,
So my soul pants for Thee, O God.

My soul thirsts for God, for the living God. . . .

PSALM 42:1–2

Those are the words of a man whose inner being ached to go to the depths. How vividly he describes his longing: "My soul pants for Thee, O God." The word picture of a deer searching for water is intriguing.

Charles Spurgeon's remarks here are beautiful:

David was heartsick. Ease he did not seek, honour he did not covet, but the enjoyment of communion with God was an urgent need of his soul . . . an absolute necessity, like water to a stag. . . . His *soul*, his very self, his deepest life, was insatiable for a sense of the divine presence. . . .

O to have the most intense craving after the highest good![2]

There is nothing—absolutely nothing—of greater importance than knowing Christ intensely and intimately. That is Paul's whole point in His words to the Philippians prior to revealing his "determined purpose."

With broad brush strokes on this autobiographical canvas, he identifies the salient accomplishments of his life:

Circumcised the eighth day,
of the nation of Israel, of the tribe of Benjamin,
a Hebrew of Hebrews; as to the Law,
a Pharisee; as to zeal, a persecutor of the church;
as to the righteousness which is in the Law,
found blameless.

PHILIPPIANS 3:5–6

Talk about impressive! But before the reader has time to ponder and begin to applaud, the writer rushes in and declares:

But whatever things were gain to me,
those things I have counted as loss
for the sake of Christ.

More than that, I count all things to be loss in
view of the surpassing value of knowing Christ
Jesus my Lord . . . and count them
but rubbish in order that I may gain Christ.

PHILIPPIANS 3:7–8

In comparison to knowing Christ deeply and intimately, he considered everything else "loss . . . rubbish." What would normally cause the public to sit up and take notice, paled into personal insignificance. Remarkable contrast!

Since that is the apostle Paul's settled and studied conviction, I suggest that we consider it an appraisal worth remembering. Frankly, in light of his testimony, I find myself encouraged to spend less energy and time pursuing all the humanly impressive accomplishments and more energy and time cultivating an intimate relationship with Christ, whom to know is life eternal. I think you feel the same.

If so, let's dig deeper.

WE

HAVE MADE

OURSELVES VERY

COMPLICATED.

FOUR DECISIONS...
FOUR DISCIPLINES

However valuable such a "determined purpose" may be, it is neither easy nor automatic. Furthermore, you and I will find no encouragement from the world's system. Isaac Watts' questions may be old, but they are painfully relevant:

Are there no foes for me to face?
Must I not stem the flood?
Is this vile world a friend to grace,
To help me on to God?[3]

During my sixty-plus years in this "vile world," with well over thirty of those years invested in the service of the Savior, I have found that there are at least four essential decisions, each related to a discipline, that assist us in cultivating an in-depth intimacy with the Almighty. Let me list the four, with the accompanying disciplines, then explain and examine them one by one.

THE DECISION	THE DISCIPLINE
to reorder one's private world	simplicity
to be still	silence
to cultivate serenity	solitude
to trust the Lord completely	surrender

If you are serious about becoming more deeply and intimately acquainted with Him, you will find these four issues to be strategic parts of the process. There are certainly *more* we could add, but not *less* than these four.

1. REORDERING ONE'S PRIVATE WORLD: THE DISCIPLINE OF SIMPLICITY

Everything around us works against reordering and simplifying our lives. Everything! Ours is a cluttered, complicated world. God did not create it that way. Depraved, restless humanity has made it that way!

> God made us plain and simple,
> but we have made ourselves
> very complicated.
>
> ECCLESIASTES 7:29 TEV

Advertisements have one major goal: to make us discontented, woefully dissatisfied with who we are and what we have. Why? So we will acquire what they offer. And acquire we do! The watchword of our consumptive society is very loud and assertive—*more!* Enough is never enough.

It isn't long before any novice in the business or religious world learns about competition, which multiplies the pressure, enlarges the expectations, and increases the speed. While competition has its benefits, who can measure the fallout that comes when it gets pushed out of control? Quotas are never enough. Relaxing the tension is never an option. Size is never sufficient. Solomon the wise is absolutely correct: "We have made ourselves very complicated."

Not only do we acquire . . . we keep, we accumulate. Furthermore, we don't simply compete . . . we are driven to win, *always* win. And not only do we want more, we must spend more time *maintaining* those things. Staying ahead of that maddening pace leaves us strained, fretful, breathless.

Surely, God is not the author of such confusion. Thomas Kelly's words come to mind. He reminds his readers that God "never guides us to an intolerable scramble of panting feverishness."[4]

To reorder one's own world, the need to simplify is imperative. Otherwise, we will find ourselves unable to be at rest within, unable to enter the deep, silent recesses of our hearts, where God's best messages are communicated. And if we live very long in that condition, our hearts grow cold toward Christ and we become objects of seduction in a wayward world. What perils await us in that condition!

I'm reminded of a warning Paul gave to his friends in busy, carnal, consumptive Corinth:

I am afraid, lest as the serpent
deceived Eve by his craftiness,
your minds should be led astray from
the simplicity and purity of
devotion to Christ.

2 CORINTHIANS 11:3

There are times I, too, feel the same fear. Being "led astray" can happen in the most unsuspected places: in a home where every member of the family is a Christian . . . in a church where truth is taught and Christ is exalted . . . even on a seminary campus where students are so busy, so pressed to produce, so exhausted from trying to maintain balance between work, studies, recreation, family needs, physical rest, and outside ministry involvements. I am afraid, I confess, that such a context might lead some astray from the very reason they enrolled at a seminary: to find contentment in

THOSE WHO

DETERMINE TO

SIMPLIFY THEIR LIVES

QUICKLY DISCOVER

IT IS A RIGOROUS SOLO

VOYAGE AGAINST

THE WIND.

simplicity and purity of devotion to Christ. How strange! On the very campus where men and women are in training to become God's messengers and servants, there are very real perils leading to the consequences of complicated living. If it can happen here, it can happen *anywhere*. Busyness is an enemy wherever it rears its ugly head.

Envy is yet another enemy of simplifying life. There is perhaps no more subtle force at work among Christians than envy even though it leads to nothing but dead-end streets. Locked into a horizontal syndrome of judging, comparing, and regretting (or feeling proud), our focus turns from the things of God and becomes riveted on others as well as ourselves. Instead of being contented (one of the wonderful by-products of simplicity), we are consumed by envy. Our standard of contentment is raised so high, we can never measure up.

I can still recall a few lines from the pen of Aleksandr Solzhenitsyn:

It is enough if you don't freeze in the cold and if thirst and hunger don't claw at your insides. If your back isn't broken, if your feet can walk, if both arms can bend, if both eyes can see, if both ears hear, then whom should you envy? And why? Our envy of others devours us most of all.[5]

So then, to reiterate the initial move toward cultivating intimacy with the Almighty, it is essential that we reorder our private lives. And that requires us to slow our pace as well as stop the envy, two tough assignments no one else can do for us. Furthermore, it is foolish to tell ourselves to sit back and wait until the winds of this world shift and blow us toward the shores of simplicity. *It ain't gonna happen!* Those who determine to simplify their lives quickly discover it is a rigorous solo voyage against the wind.

To paraphrase a poet:

One ship drives east and
another drives west
With the selfsame winds that blow.
'Tis the set of the sails
And not the gales
Which tells us the way to go.[6]

To get rid of the clutter, simplicity isn't just nice—it's essential. But neither is it automatic; it will call forth intense determination.

2. BEING STILL: THE DISCIPLINE OF SILENCE

The list gets tougher, not easier. If you think it is a difficult test in our complicated, competitive world, to develop the discipline of simplicity, just imagine the challenge you face in this world of restlessness, noise, words, and relentless activity, to develop the discipline of silence. Personally, I have found this to be an almost insurmountable challenge. I've realized its magnitude more in the

BE STILL
AND KNOW
THAT I AM
GOD.

past two years than ever before in my life. Yet, I am more convinced than ever that there is no way you and I can move toward a deeper, intimate relationship with our God without protracted times of stillness, which includes one of the rarest of all experiences: absolute silence.

Am I sounding more like a mystical dreamer? If so, so was the psalmist who wrote those familiar words we often quote but seldom obey, "Be still and know that I am God" (Ps. 46:10, NIV). Before hurrying past that profound command, let's turn it over in our minds several times.

> *Cease striving and know that I am God.*
> *Stand silent! Know that I am God!* [TLB]

> *Let be and be still, and know—recognize and*
> *understand—that I am God.* [AMP]

> *"Give in," he cries,*
> *"admit that I am God."* [Moffat]

> *"Stop fighting," he says,*
> *"and know that I am God."* [TEV]

I am especially intrigued by the creative paraphrase employed by Eugene Peterson:

*Step out of the traffic! Take a long, loving
look at me, your High God, above politics,
above everything.* [THE MESSAGE]

However we may prefer to read it, this is an
emphatic imperative addressed to God's own
people. People of every race, color, culture, and
era . . . people of any level of maturity and age . . .
people who are employed or unemployed, single
or married, with or without children, all people
whose God is the Lord.

We are commanded to stop (literally) . . . rest,
relax, let go, and make time for Him. The scene is
one of stillness and quietness, listening and waiting
before Him. Such foreign experiences in these
busy times! Nevertheless, knowing God deeply
and intimately requires such discipline. Silence is
indispensable if we hope to add depth to our spiritual life. It "guards the fire within our souls," . . .

Noise and
words and frenzied,
hectic schedules
dull our senses, closing
our ears to His still,
small voice and
making us numb to
His touch.

"silence makes us pilgrims,"[7] writes one who advocates protracted, uninterrupted periods of quietness. It sharpens the keen edge of our souls, sensitizing us to those ever-so-slight nudgings from our heavenly Father. Noise and words and frenzied, hectic schedules dull our senses, closing our ears to His still, small voice and making us numb to His touch.

Roman Catholic priest, scholar, and author, Henri Nouwen, does a splendid job of analyzing then illustrating the downside of what he calls "our wordy world."

> There was a time not too long ago without radios and televisions, stop signs, yield signs, merge signs, bumper stickers, and the ever-present announcements indicating price increases or special sales. There was a time without the advertisements which now cover whole cities with words.
>
> Recently I was driving through Los Angeles,

NOISE AND
CROWDS HAVE A WAY
OF SIPHONING OUR ENERGY
AND DISTRACTING OUR
ATTENTION, MAKING
PRAYER AN ADDED CHORE
RATHER THAN
A COMFORTING RELIEF.

and suddenly I had the strange sensation of driving through a huge dictionary. Wherever I looked there were words trying to take my eyes from the road. They said, "Use me, take me, buy me, drink me, smell me, touch me, kiss me, sleep with me." In such a world who can maintain respect for words?[8]

My response? Been there—done that! For almost twenty-five years my family and I lived in the Los Angeles area. On the one hand, they were years of incredible freedom, growth, and blessing. For those things I remain eternally grateful. But, on the other hand, I must confess that I found myself becoming weary of the noise, the crowds, the pace, the relentless press of activities, the never-ending rush of traffic. While we thoroughly enjoyed the people, the opportunities for ministry, and certainly the weather of that area of the country, there were times we ached for relief . . . for the essential presence of stillness, of silence.

I can remember occasions when we would escape to the mountains, only an hour-and-a-half removed from the blare of horns, the roar of traffic, and other loud sounds of a busy city. Sitting together up there, often leaning against a giant Ponderosa pine or age-old oak, we would invariably comment on the therapy of stillness. The wind whistling through the leaves along with little squirrels scampering up the trunk of a twisted tree, then later in the year, watching soft, falling snow blanket the ground with white . . . such quiet visits with nature never failed to draw our hearts closer to our God. I can honestly say, such extended visits with silence invariably made us more sensitive to spiritual things, more appreciative of God's presence and grace. In a word, they made us *deeper.*

So much for me. What about you? Do you find yourself victimized by the noisy, busy, over-crowded world in which you must spend many hours of your life? Is it leaving you spiritually insensitive, sort of a business-as-usual attitude toward the church you attend or the Bible study you used to enjoy? How about prayer? Noise and crowds have a way of siphoning our energy and distracting our attention, making prayer an added chore rather than a comforting relief. You may even feel a low-grade depression sweep over you as the absence of stillness and silence takes its toll.

If so, it is time for some straight talk. Nobody can do anything about that dilemma *but you!* Allow it to continue, and you will gravitate into one of two directions. Either you will run through the motions and cultivate a hypocritical spirituality hidden behind the mask of phony enthusiasm, or you will simply fade from involvement and distance yourself from meaningful relationships with other Christians. In both cases, you will set yourself up for a fall. I have seen it happen more often than I want to recall.

It is easy for us to be sucked into a sort of black hole of activities in these hurried times. As that happens, we find ourselves running from others in our own family rather than toward them. The results can be disastrous.

Dolores Curran points out:

In an incisive article called "Fast Folk," which appeared in . . . *Harpers*, Louis T. Grant dissects an article published earlier in *Woman's Day* in which the life-style of one working mother is praised and presented as a model of sorts. Listen to this woman's life. She rushes from home to work in the morning, eating yogurt in the car for break-fast; has lunch at the spa where she works out; leaves child care to her husband, who also has a managerial position forty miles the other side of home; pilots a small plane in her leisure time for pleasure; teaches on the side a class at a local women's college; leaves the kids with Grandma; leaves the kids with sitters; leaves the kids. . . . Grant

IF THE PACE

AND THE PUSH, THE

NOISE AND THE CROWDS

ARE GETTING TO YOU,

IT'S TIME TO STOP THE

NONSENSE AND FIND

A PLACE OF SOLACE TO

REFRESH YOUR SPIRIT.

likens this life-style, which he calls "fast folk," to keeping up with the gerbils. In his immensely perceptive piece, he illustrates the shallowness of relationships in a fast-folk family. There's no time in such a family for one another, for intimacy, for communication, for listening. That's for slowpokes. And, the author points out, "children are slowpokes."[9]

Make no mistake here. If that comes anywhere near your lifestyle these days, *it's your move!* If the pace and the push, the noise and the crowds are getting to you, it's time to stop the nonsense and find a place of solace to refresh your spirit. Deliberately say "no" more often. This will leave room for you to slow down, get alone, pour out your overburdened heart, and admit your desperate need for inner refreshment. The good news is He will hear and He will help. The bad news is this: If you wait for someone else to bring about a change, things will only deteriorate. Your spiritual fervor will wane and you will be vulnerable to an adversarial assault, which will surely come. Strengthening yourself before the Lord is your only hope.

I'm reminded of a vivid scene from the life of David before he became the king in Israel. He and his men had been engaged in a nonstop series of events in Philistine territory. On top of all that was the ever-increasing assault of Saul, whose jealousy of David had resulted in more than a dozen years of cat-and-mouse pursuit. Just imagine the pressure.

Following a three-day trip home to their families in Ziklag, David and his fellow warriors came upon a horrible sight. Prior to the soldiers' return, the Amalekites had raided their village, burned it to the ground, and kidnapped all their wives and children. Read the tragic account and picture the sad scene in your mind:

Then it happened when David and his men came to Ziklag on the third day, that the Amalekites had made a raid on the Negev and on Ziklag,

and had overthrown Ziklag and burned it with
fire; and they took captive the women and all
who were in it, both small and great, without
killing anyone, and carried them off and went
their way. And when David and his men came to
the city, behold, it was burned with fire, and
their wives and their sons and their daughters
had been taken captive. Then David and the
people who were with him lifted their voices and
wept until there was no strength in them to weep.

1 SAMUEL 30:1–4

As if that were not enough, in the hysteria
and depression of their chaos—

The people spoke of stoning [David], for all the
people were embittered, each one because of his
sons and daughters . . . (v. 6a).

Just imagine! On top of the unending pressure from Saul, the exhaustion from battle, the
loss of their homes, and the intense concern for

the safety of their families, murmurings of mutiny spread like cancer throughout the camp.

No one came to David's defense or rescue. Few have ever felt more alone, but no one ever rose to the occasion more responsibly or more maturely. We read his secret in a few words: "David strengthened himself in the LORD his God" (v. 6b).

Don't miss the point—David faced the situation with realism; but he refused to panic, to fight back, to run, or to dissolve in self-pity. Realizing his dire need for time alone with God, he moved away from his embittered companions, away from that chaotic scene, and sought a place of quietness and stillness to strengthen his soul.

Intimacy with the Almighty calls for disciplines that are no longer valued or emulated by the majority today. To begin with, there must be simplicity, which allows us the room to reorder our private world. Then, there must be silence, a rarity in our times. Silence, as we've seen in Scripture, makes our moments of stillness meaningful.

Several months ago as my wife, Cynthia, and I were searching to know more of the Father's will for our future, I became nervous. In that unsettled state of mind, I entertained fearful, anxious thoughts. My imagination ran wild, causing a rush of panic to occupy my mind. It wasn't long before I felt exhausted and confused, virtually immobilized.

She and I were committed to travel abroad and to be involved in a week of meetings. I was tempted to cancel, due to the harassed condition of my soul. Thankfully, I didn't . . . for it was during a meal before one of those meetings that someone unexpectedly handed me a profound paragraph that brought quietness to my heart and settled my spirit. I knew nothing about the original source or the author, except that his words resonated with my spirit deeply and directly.

As you read it, you will understand why it ministered to me in such a meaningful manner.

Harassed by life, exhausted, we look about us for somewhere to be quiet, to be genuine, a place of refreshment. We yearn to restore our spirits in God, to simply let go in him and gain new strength to go on living. But we fail to look for him where he is waiting for us, where he is to be found: in his Son, who is his Word. Or else we seek for God because there are a thousand things we want to ask him, and imagine that we cannot go on living unless they are answered. *We inundate him with problems, with demands for information, for clues, for an easier path, forgetting that in his Word he has given us the solution to every problem and all the details we are capable of grasping in this life.* We fail to listen where God speaks: where God's Word rang out in the world once for all, sufficient for all ages, inexhaustible. Or else we think that God's Word has been heard on earth for so long that by now it is almost used up, that it is about time for some new word, as if we had the right to demand one. We fail to see that it is we ourselves who are used up and alienated, whereas the Word resounds with the same vitality and freshness as ever; it is just as near to us as it always was.[10]

As all of us can testify, God does not speak to the hurried, worried mind. It takes time alone with Him and His Word before we can expect our spiritual strength to recover. That particular thought leads us to a third priority if we hope to have an intimate relationship with the Almighty.

3. CULTIVATING SERENITY: THE DISCIPLINE OF SOLITUDE

As invaluable and necessary as companionship is, enabling us to be encouraged, accountable, and challenged, there is an equally important segment of the spiritual life that is frequently ignored. I'm referring to the discipline of *solitude*, where we cultivate serenity deep within ourselves.

Soul surgery

transpires as

serenity replaces

anxiety.

Solitude has been called "the furnace of transformation."[11] I don't have in mind mere personal privacy for a twelve-second pit stop where we get a quick fix to reenter the race. It is more than that. It is an oasis of the soul where we see ourselves, others, and especially our God in new ways. It is where much of the "clutter" I mentioned earlier is identified and exterminated, thanks to the merciless heat of the "furnace." Soul surgery transpires as serenity replaces anxiety.

In solitude, struggles occur that no one else knows about. Inner battles are fought here that seldom become fodder for sermons or illustrations for books. God, who probes our deepest thoughts during protracted segments of solitude, opens our eyes to things that need attention. It is here He makes us aware of those things we try to hide from others.

Henri Nouwen describes solitude in practical, searching terms:

In solitude I get rid of my scaffolding: no friends to talk with, no telephone calls to make, no meetings to attend, no music to entertain, no books to distract, just me— naked, vulnerable, weak, sinful, deprived, broken—nothing. It is this nothingness that I have to face in my solitude, a nothingness so dreadful that everything in me wants to run to my friends, my work, and my distractions so that I can forget my nothingness and make myself believe that I am worth something. But that is not all. As soon as I decide to stay in my solitude, confusing ideas, disturbing images, wild fantasies, and weird associations jump about in my mind like monkeys in a banana tree. Anger and greed begin to show their ugly faces. . . .

The task is to persevere in my solitude, to stay in my cell until all my seductive visitors get tired of pounding on my door and leave me alone.[12]

GOD, WHO

PROBES OUR DEEPEST

THOUGHTS DURING

PROTRACTED SEGMENTS

OF SOLITUDE, OPENS OUR

EYES TO THINGS THAT

NEED ATTENTION.

If the truth were known, most of us resist that kind of soul searching because it seems too radical, too severe. After all, time is short, and who needs all that kind of self-analysis? The religious show must go on! No, that's just the point. Through the discipline of solitude, we come to terms with the superficial "show," and we determine in our hearts that it will stop!

The psalmist realized the need for in-depth examination. In fact, he invited God's laserlike probe into the innermost chambers of his heart and thoughts.

O LORD, Thou hast searched me
and known me.
Thou dost know when I sit down
and when I rise up;
Thou dost understand my
thought from afar.
Thou dost scrutinize my path
and my lying down,

And art intimately acquainted
with all my ways.
Even before there is a word
on my tongue,
Behold, O LORD, thou dost
know it all. . . .
Search me, O God, and know my heart;
Try me and know my anxious thoughts;
And see if there be any hurtful
way in me,
And lead me in the everlasting way.

PSALM 139:1–4, 23–24

Paul was equally committed to solitude and self-analysis. Without hesitation he admonished the Corinthians for their shameful sham at the Lord's Table when they met corporately.

> *But in giving this instruction, I do not praise you,*
> *because you come together not for the better but*
> *for the worse. For, in the first place, when you come*
> *together as a church, I hear that divisions exist*

How busy

WE HAVE BECOME . . .

AND AS A RESULT,

HOW EMPTY!

among you; and in part, I believe it. For there must
also be factions among you, in order that those
who are approved may have become evident
among you. Therefore when you meet together, it is
not to eat the Lord's Supper, for in your eating
each one takes his own supper first; and one is
hungry and another is drunk. What! Do you not
have houses in which to eat and drink? Or do you
despise the church of God, and shame those who
have nothing? What shall I say to you? Shall I
praise you? In this I will not praise you.

1 Corinthians 11:17–22

He then instructed each one to spend time in
solitude and personal, unassisted self-examination
before the Lord:

But let a man examine himself, and so let him
eat of the bread and drink of the cup. For he who
eats and drinks, eats and drinks judgment to
himself, if he does not judge the body rightly. For

this reason many among you are weak and sick,
and a number sleep. But if we judged ourselves
rightly, we should not be judged.

1 CORINTHIANS 11:28–31

An inner restlessness grows within us
when we refuse to get alone and examine our
own hearts, including our motives. As our lives
begin to pick up the debris that accompanies a
lot of activities and involvements, we can train
ourselves to go right on, to stay active, to be
busy in the Lord's work. Unless we discipline
ourselves to pull back, to get alone for the hard
work of self-examination in times of solitude,
serenity will remain only a distant dream. How
busy we can become . . . and as a result, how
empty! We mouth words, but they mean nothing. We find ourselves trafficking in unlived
truths. We fake spirituality.

One of my favorite statements of the late A.
W. Tozer is never far from my thoughts:

May not the inadequacy of much of our spiritual experience be traced back to our habit of skipping through the corridors of the Kingdom like children in the market place, chattering about everything, but pausing to learn the true value of nothing?[13]

It's time for judgment to begin in the house of God. Let's admit it, you and I know of few places more susceptible to empty and endless chatter than religious circles. How easy to fall prey to meaningless talk, cliché-ridden responses, and mindless activities! It was never meant to be that way; but, more often than not, that's the way it is. To break the habit, solitude is required. The hard work of self-examination on a recurring basis is absolutely essential.

Do you remember Jesus' response to His disciples immediately on the heels of their ministry? Read and take notice:

And the apostles gathered together with Jesus;
and they reported to Him all that they had
done and taught. And He said to them, "Come
away by yourselves to a lonely place and rest a
while." (For there were many people coming and
going, and they did not even have time to eat.)
And they went away in the boat to a lonely
place by themselves.

MARK 6:30–32

While our Lord appreciated their hard work and faithful labors as they returned from ministry on their own, He saw their need for rest and reflection. He was well-acquainted with the draining influence of "many people coming and going" (sounds like the scene after most church services), so He encouraged them to slip away as He got them in a boat and sailed with them to "a lonely place." Why? So they could be in a place "by themselves." Clearly, Jesus saw the value of solitude . . . the need for escape from activity. It was there that serenity could be cultivated.

Before proceeding to the last of the four disciplines, let me pause to share with you something that has added immensely to my own times of solitude and self-examination: keeping a journal. I have been doing this for years, and the benefits are more than most would believe. Unlike a Daytimer or simply a diary, a journal is a splendid way to spend time alone remembering and recording God's dealings in your life. While enjoying times of solitude, it is easy to think that the thoughts or insights He reveals will stay in your mind forever. Not so. It isn't long before they are submerged under the load of responsibilities and conversations. Activities erase deep and meaningful thoughts. But they're too important for that to happen.

Furthermore, our journal entries give us rallying points . . . historical, dated markers that specify God's dealings deep within our souls as well as His workings on our behalf. We need to preserve a written record of such divine interventions. The use of a journal can make times of solitude extremely meaningful. Periodically, I review at random a few of those hundreds of pages. Without exception, I am humbled and strengthened to see how obviously His hand has been at the helm of my life, even though at certain times He may have seemed distant and disinterested. As that hindsight perspective occurs, serenity returns and calms my spirit. I want to restate that a journal is not a daily diary; it is an intimate record of the journey that the Lord and I are traveling together. His presence is seen and felt page after page after page.

I heartily recommend that you begin to keep a journal, especially if you find yourself "scatter-shooting" rather than focusing in times of solitude.

4. Trusting the Lord Completely: The Discipline of Surrender

I am aware that "trusting the Lord" sounds neither new nor creative. In fact, some see those words as nothing more than a meaningless and tired cliché.

That need not be so. Reminders to trust in the Lord appear numerous times in the Scriptures, but never more significantly than in Proverbs 3:5–6:

> Trust in the LORD with all your heart,
> And do not lean on your
> own understanding.
> In all your ways acknowledge Him,
> And He will make your
> paths straight.

I'm not the first to observe that this command "trust in the Lord" is no half-hearted hope of a reluctant heart. On the contrary, it is a conscious acknowledgment of Him "in all your ways."

Anyone whose determined purpose is to become more deeply and intimately acquainted with Him cannot retain the rights to his own position or place . . . or be anxiously preoccupied

SURRENDER. . .

IS THE KEY THAT

UNLOCKS THE

VAULT OF GOD'S

BEST AND DEEPEST

TREASURES.

with working out the details of his own life. There must be complete and unqualified reliance on the Living Lord. In other words, one must develop the discipline of surrender.

Now, *there's* an unpopular term for today's generation! I can just hear the frowning reaction. "Surrender? Get serious." Who is encouraged to surrender anything these days? If I were to name a few areas, these are the answers I'd hear:

Surrender your rights.	"Are you kidding? I'll sue!"
Surrender your future.	"No way. My mind's made up!"
Surrender your will.	"Not me. I give in to no one!"
Surrender your dreams.	"Never. I've worked too hard!"
Surrender to your mate.	"Me? Get a life!"
Surrender your finances.	"What? I'm planning to retire!"

We have reared a generation of strong-willed, belligerent, independent young men and women. Surrender is not a word in their vocabulary. Too bad, since it is the key that unlocks the vault of God's best and deepest treasures. He patiently waits for us to yield, to quit fighting Him, to allow His plan to run its course, to turn to Him for our security and significance. As He witnesses our doing that, He begins to reveal Himself and His will in greater depth.

Over the years I have known the Lord, I have observed that surrendering my will to His way was much more difficult early on. When I was younger, I often said I wanted His plan to run its course; but I resisted it more often than I care to remember, especially when it included unexpected detours and disappointments. Finally, at long last, after I got weary of running into the consequences of my self-made world, I slowly realized His way was best.

I shook my head with understanding when I read the following words in a book I've come to

NOTHING

UNDER HIS CONTROL

CAN EVER BE OUT

OF CONTROL.

appreciate. I've not read anything that better describes the give-and-take struggle of my early years as a Christian. They are words from a collection of Puritan prayers and devotions.

When thou wouldst guide me
I control myself.
When thou wouldst be sovereign
I rule myself.
When thou wouldst take care of me
I suffice myself.
When I should depend on thy providings
I supply myself.
When I should submit to thy providence
I follow my will.
When I should study, honour, trust thee,
I serve myself;
I fault and correct thy laws
to suit myself,
Instead of thee I look to
man's approbation,

and am by nature an idolater.
Lord, it is my chief design
to bring my heart back to Thee.[14]

That is the honest confession of an unsurrendered life. The heartbreak is that though his words are dated, he describes far too many who are in God's family this very day.

In order to end this book on a positive note, I want to affirm the importance of relinquishing everything to Him because He is *fully trustworthy.* I am finally learning this; it is no longer something I verbalize from a pulpit or write in a book. I'm finally learning that His sovereign plan is the best plan. That whatever I entrust to Him, He can take care of better than I. That nothing under His control can ever be out of control. That everything I need, He knows about in every detail. That He is able to supply, to guide, to start, to stop, to sustain, to change, and to correct in His time and for His purposes. When I keep my hands out of things, His will is accomplished, His Name is exalted, and His glory is magnified.

Why it took me so long to realize these things is a mystery. It is a testimony to His grace that He has allowed me to live long enough to see them clearly and to embrace them whole-heartedly.

I am finally learning that surrendering to my sovereign Lord, leaving the details of my future in His hands, is the most responsible act of obedience I can do. And, *until* I do it, becoming a deep person remains nothing more than a distant and pious dream.

WHEN I KEEP MY

HANDS OUT OF THINGS,

HIS WILL

IS ACCOMPLISHED,

HIS NAME IS EXALTED,

AND HIS GLORY

IS MAGNIFIED.

CONCLUSION

T his has been an intriguing journey. As I mentioned at the beginning, deep things are intriguing.

I have spent only a few pages outlining four decisions, accompanied by four disciplines, that can lead us into a deeper, more intimate relationship with the Almighty. If they are taken seriously and practiced consistently, I am convinced they will make a profound difference in our spiritual walk. Without them, however, superficiality will continue to characterize our lives.

In summary, these are the decisions and the disciplines we have been considering:

1. To reorder our private world, we must learn to exercise the discipline of *simplicity*.

2. To be still, the discipline of *silence* must be valued.

3. To cultivate serenity, it is imperative that we guard the discipline of *solitude*.

4. To trust God completely requires the discipline of *surrender*.

I have no way of knowing whose hands will someday hold this book . . . or whose life may be redirected because of it. Those things are all in God's hands and under His care; therefore, I leave it all with Him. By His grace He will bring these words to a few lives who genuinely hunger and thirst after righteousness. I have no idea who those people will be.

But I am sure of this: Some who read and wrestle with these things will need the reminder that it is time to put on the brakes and clear out the clutter . . . it is time to pause and listen, to be quiet and learn, to get alone and release whatever is hindering the Father's perfect way.

For your sake especially, I close with the tender words from a man who modeled these things as a servant-hearted leader during his earthly life,

THE PAUSE

AND THE HUSH SING

A DOUBLE SONG. . .

BE STILL

AND KNOW!

and who is now enjoying a face-to-face, in-depth relationship with his Master in the uninterrupted glories of heaven.

> In every life
> There's a pause that is better than
> 　　onward rush,
> Better than hewing or mightiest doing;
> 'Tis the standing still at Sovereign will.
>
> There's a hush that is better
> 　　than ardent speech,
> Better than sighing or wilderness crying;
> 'Tis the being still at Sovereign will.
>
> The pause and the hush sing
> 　　a double song
> In unison low and for all time long.
> O human soul, God's working plan
> Goes on, nor needs the aid of man!
> Stand still, and see!
> Be still, and know![15]

NOTES

1.   Richard J. Foster, *Celebration of Discipline* (San Francisco: Harper & Row, 1978) 1.

2.   C. H. Spurgeon, *The Treasury of David*, vol. 2 (McLean, Vir.: Macdonald Publishing Company, nd) 270, 271.

3.   Isaac Watts, "Am I a Soldier of the Cross?"

4.   Thomas Kelly, *A Testament of Devotion* (New York: Harper & Row Publishers, 1941) 124.

5.   Aleksandr Solzhenitsyn, *The Gulag Archipelago*. Trans. Thomas P. Whitney (New York: Harper & Row, 1973) 591–92.

6.   Ella Wheeler Wilcox, "The Wind of Fate," in *The Best Loved Poems of the American People*. Comp. Hazel Felleman (Garden City, New York: Garden City Books; copyright, 1936, by Doubleday & Company, Inc.) 364.

7.   Henri J. M. Nouwen, *The Way of the Heart*. (N.Y.: The Seabury Press, 1981) 52, 50.

8.   Ibid., 45–46.

9.   Dolores Curran, *Traits of a Healthy Family* (Minneapolis, Minn.: Winston, Press, 1983) 117–18.

10. Hans Ur von Balthasar, *Prayer.* Trans. Graham Harrison (San Francisco: Ignatius Press, 1986) 16.

11. Nouwen, *The Way of the Heart*, 25.

12. Ibid., 27, 28.

13. A. W. Tozer, *The Divine Conquest* (Camp Hill, Penn.: Christian Publications 1950; copyright renewed 1978, Lowell Tozer) 22.

14. Arthur Bennett, ed., *The Valley of Vision* (Carlisle, Penn.: The Banner of Truth Trust, 1975) 91.

15. V. Raymond Edman, *The Disciplines of Life* (Wheaton, Ill.: Scripture Press, 1948) 83.

NOISE AN

and frenzied

DULL

SE

closing ou

HIS STILL, SMALL V